GREAT BASIN NATIONAL PARK
ACTIVITY BOOK

PUZZLES, MAZES, GAMES, AND MORE ABOUT GREAT BASIN NATIONAL PARK

NATIONAL PARKS ACTIVITIES SERIES

GREAT BASIN NATIONAL PARK ACTIVITY BOOK

Copyright 2022
Published by Little Bison Press

The author acknowledges that the land on which Great Basin National Park is located are the traditional lands of the Goshute Tribe.

LITTLE BISON
Press

For more free national parks activities, visit
www.littlebisonpress.com

About Great Basin National Park

Great Basin National Park is located in the state of Nevada and was established as a national park in 1986. In this wild and rugged landscape, it holds incredible things to do. People come from all over the world to experience the pristine nighttime environment - perfect for viewing celestial bodies such as stars, planets, meteors, and star clusters! The skies here are some of the darkest in the United States.

Besides stargazing, the park is famous for the Great Basin Bristlecone Pine, a grove of ancient trees. These trees are an extremely rare species found only in California, Nevada, and Utah. They grow in harsh, high-elevation environments where few other things live.

Guests to the park can also visit the Lehman Caves at the base of 13,063-foot Wheeler Peak, a huge cave system with an interesting history. Year-round, visitors to Great Basin National Park can reserve a ranger-led tour through the Lehman Caves, where park rangers explain the history, ecology, and geology of the caves.

Great Basin National Park is famous for:
- Groves of bristlecone pines
- Lehman Caves
- Astronomy

Hey, I'm Parker!

I'm the only snail in history to visit every National Park in the United States! Come join me on my adventures in Great Basin National Park.

Throughout this book, we will learn about the history of the park, the animals and plants that live here, and things to do if you ever visit in person. This book is also full of games and activities!

Last but not least, I am hidden 9 times on different pages. See how many times you can find me. This page doesn't count!

Great Basin Bingo

Let's play bingo! Cross off each box you are able to during your visit to the national park. Try to get a bingo down, across, or diagonally. If you can't visit the park, use the bingo board to plan your perfect trip.

Pick out some activities you would want to do during your visit. What would you do first? How long would you spend there? What animals would you try to see?

TAKE A RIDE UP THE WHEELER PEAK SCENIC DRIVE	SEE A MOUNTAIN	GO FOR A HIKE	TAKE A PICTURE AT AN OVERLOOK	WATCH A MOVIE AT THE VISITORS CENTER
IDENTIFY A TREE	LEARN ABOUT THE INDIGENOUS PEOPLE WHO LIVE IN THIS AREA	WITNESS A SUNRISE OR SUNSET	OBSERVE THE NIGHT SKIES	GO WILDFLOWER VIEWING
HEAR A BIRD CALL	SEE SOME SNOW	FREE SPACE	LEARN ABOUT THE IMPORTANCE OF THE NIGHT SKY	SPOT SOME ANIMAL TRACKS
PICK UP TEN PIECES OF TRASH	HAVE A PICNIC	SEE A MULE DEER	VISIT THE LEHMAN CAVES	SPOT A BIRD OF PREY
LEARN ABOUT THE GEOLOGY OF THE SIERRA NEVADAS	SEE SOMEONE RIDING A HORSE	GO CAMPING	VISIT A RANGER STATION	PARTICIPATE IN A RANGER-LED ACTIVITY

Design a Set of Stickers

Imagine you have been hired to design a sticker set that will be for sale in the national park gift shop. These stickers will be a souvenir for visitors to put on water bottles, notebooks, laptops, and more.

You could include a plant or animal that lives here, the park name, and the year it was established, or a famous place in the park or activity you can do while visiting. Make sure to use colors you think represent the park!

Take a Hike

Go for a hike with your friends or family. If you aren't able to visit Great Basin National Park, go for a walk in a park near where you live. Read through the prompts before your walk and finish the activities after you return.

Draw something you saw that moves:

Draw something you saw when you looked up:

Draw something you saw that grows out of the ground:

Draw a picture of your favorite part of the walk:

Rock Scavenger Hunt

Pay close attention to the things beneath your feet. If you visit Great Basin National Park, you will see all sorts of rocks, both big and small. Go on a rock hunt!
You may have to get close to the ground and focus carefully to be able to find all the rocks on this list.

☐ A sharp rock   ☐ A smooth rock

☐ A flat rock   ☐ A small rock

☐ A round rock   ☐ A huge rock

☐ A rectangular rock   ☐ A rough rock

☐ A dull rock   ☐ A shiny rock

☐ A striped rock   ☐ A speckled rock

☐ A multicolored rock   ☐ A rock with only one color

Compare two rocks that look very different from each other.
What makes them different? Think about their size, their shape, their texture, and their color.
Do they have any similarities?

_____

_____

_____

Go Horseback Riding on the Bristlecone Grove

Help find the horse's lost shoe!

start here →

DID YOU KNOW?

Horseback riding is a popular activity in Great Basin National Park. There are many trails that you can take horses for day or overnight trips.

The National Park Logo

The National Park System has over 400 units in the US. Just like Great Basin National Park, each location is unique or special in some way. The areas include other national parks, historic sites, monuments, seashores, and other recreation areas.

Each element of the National Park emblem represents something that the National Park Service protects. Fill in each blank below to show what each symbol represents.

WORD BANK:

MOUNTAINS, ARROWHEAD, BISON, SEQUOIA TREE, WATER

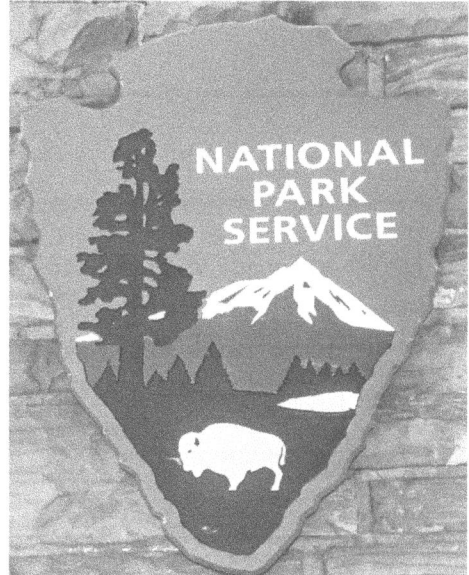

This represents all plants: _____

This represents all animals: _____

This represents the landscapes: _____

This represents the waters protected by the park service: _____

This represents the historical and archeological values: _____

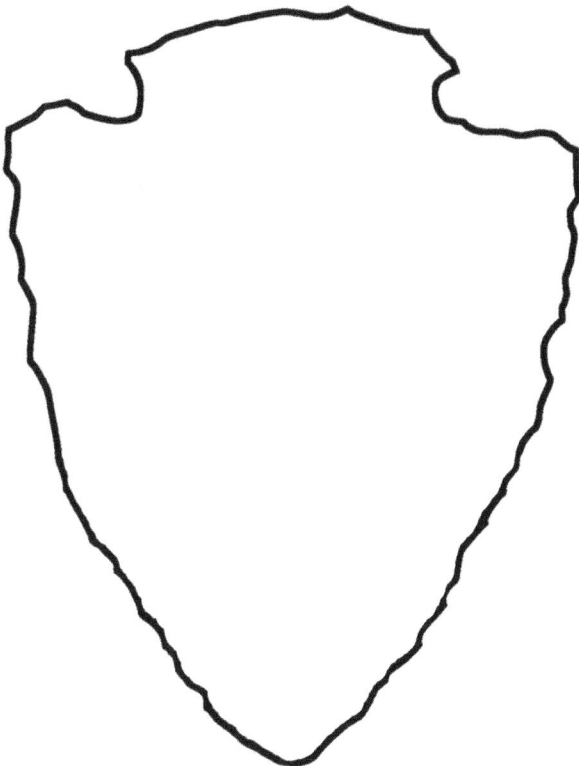

Now it's your turn! Pretend you are designing a new national park. Add elements to the design that represent the things your park protects.

What is the name of your park?

Describe why you included the symbols that you chose. What do they mean?

Great Basin National Park

Date: _____

Season: _____

Who I went with: _____

Weather: _____

How was your experience? Write a few sentences about your trip. Where did you stay? What did you do? What was your favorite activity? If you haven't visited the park yet, write a paragraph pretending that you did.

_____

_____

_____

_____

_____

_____

STAMPS

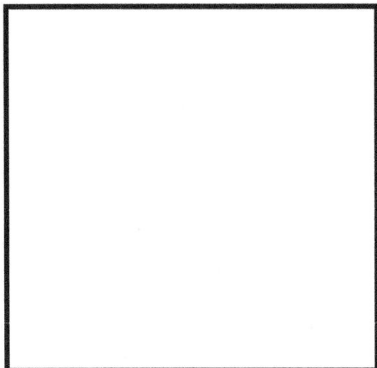

Many national parks and monuments have cancellation stamps for visitors to use. These rubber stamps record the date and location that you visited. Many people collect the markings as a free souvenir. Check with a ranger to see where you can find a stamp during your visit. If you aren't able to find one, you can draw your own.

Where is the Park?

Great Basin National Park is in the northwest United States. It is located in Eastern Nevada near the Utah border. Nevada has been nicknamed the Silver State because of the important role this metal has played in Nevada's history.

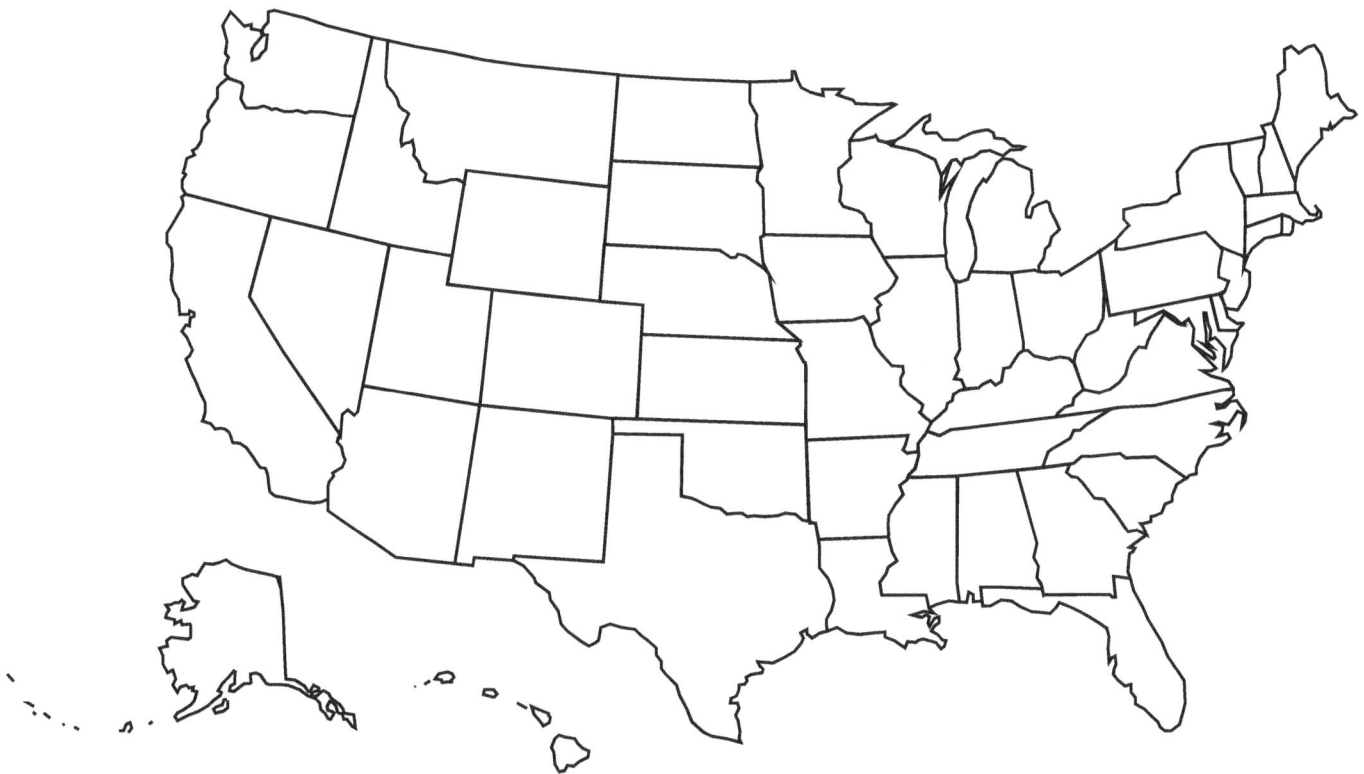

Nevada

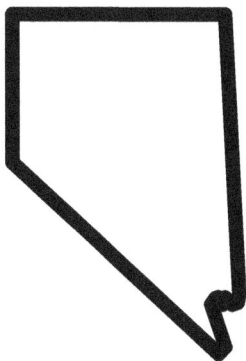

Look at the shape of Nevada. Can you find it on the map? If you are from the US, can you find your home state? Color Nevada red. Put a star on the map where you live.

Connect the Dots

Connect the dots to figure out what this tiny critter is. There are five types of these that live in Great Basin National Park.

29 1
28
2
26
27
7
6 8 9 10
3 5 11
12
4 13
25
24 23
14
22
15
16
21 17
20 18
19

Their heart rate can reach as high as 1,260 beats per minute and a breathing rate of 250 breaths per minute. Have you ever measured your breathing rate? Ask a friend or family member to set a timer for 60 seconds. Once they say "go," try to breathe normally. Count each breath until they say "stop." How do your breaths per minute compare to hummingbirds?

_____

_____

Protecting the Park

When you visit national parks, it is important to leave the park the way you found it. Did you know that the national parks get hundreds of millions of visitors every year? We can only protect national parks for future visitors to enjoy if everyone does their part. The choices each visitor makes when visiting the park have a big impact all together.

Read each line below. Write a sentence or draw a picture to show the impacts these changes would make on the park.

What would happen if every visitor fed the wild animals?

What would happen if every visitor picked a flower?

What would happen if every visitor took home a few rocks?

What would happen if every visitor wrote or carved their name on the rocks or trees?

Who Lives Here?

Below are 10 plants and animals that live in the park.
Use the word bank to fill in the clues below.

WORD BANK: PORCUPINE, PYGMY RABBIT, HOARY BAT, BIGHORN SHEEP,
WESTERN SKINK, RINGTAIL, MALLARD, RATTLESNAKE,
KILLDEER, GRAY FOX

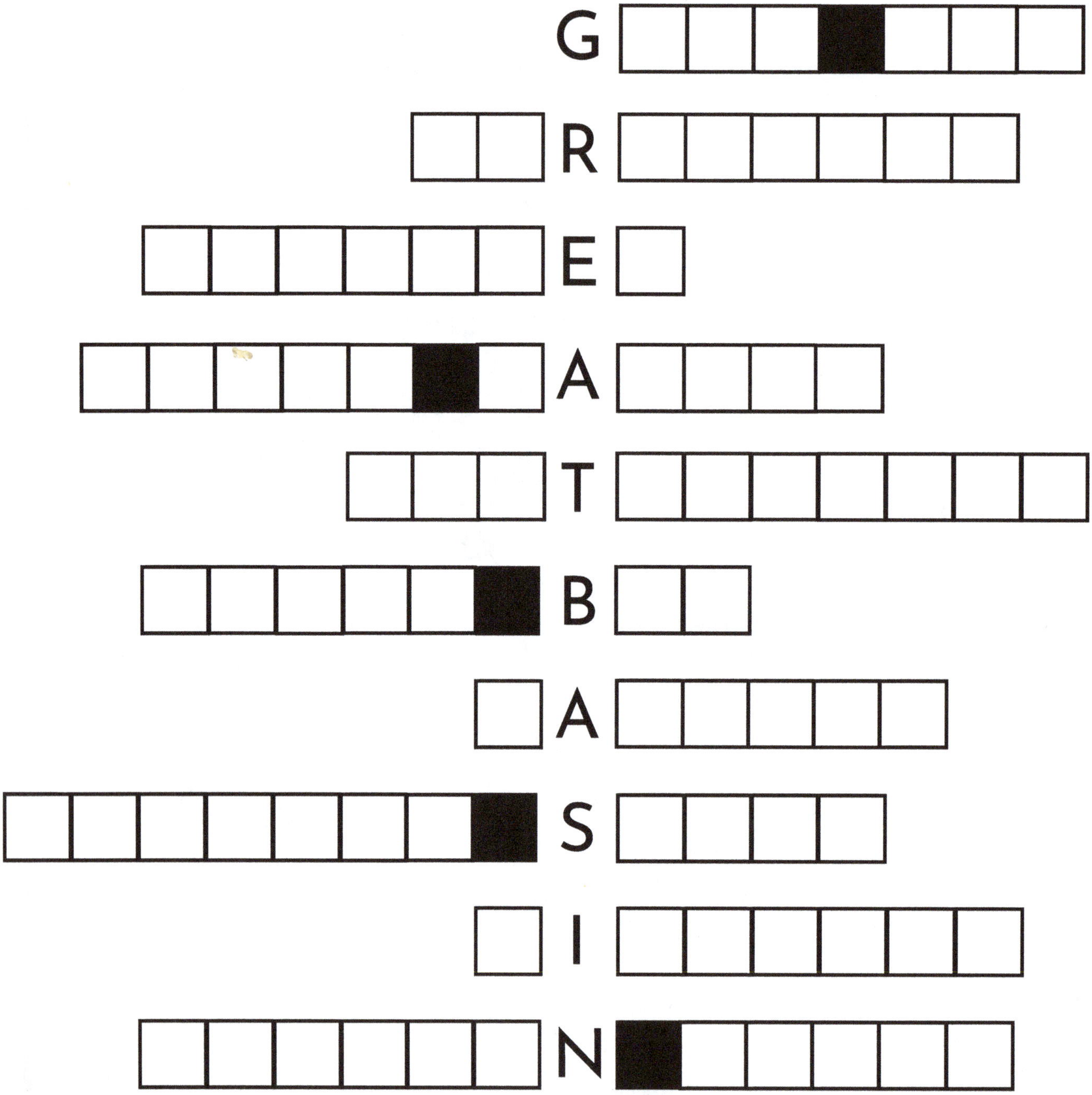

G ☐ ☐ ☐ ■ ☐ ☐ ☐

☐ ☐ R ☐ ☐ ☐ ☐ ☐ ☐

☐ ☐ ☐ ☐ ☐ E ☐

☐ ☐ ☐ ☐ ■ ☐ A ☐ ☐ ☐ ☐

☐ ☐ ☐ T ☐ ☐ ☐ ☐ ☐ ☐

☐ ☐ ☐ ☐ ■ B ☐ ☐

☐ A ☐ ☐ ☐ ☐

☐ ☐ ☐ ☐ ☐ ☐ ■ S ☐ ☐ ☐

☐ I ☐ ☐ ☐ ☐ ☐

☐ ☐ ☐ ☐ ☐ N ■ ☐ ☐ ☐ ☐

Animals of Great Basin National Park

Beavers
are the largest North American rodent.

Porcupines
are well known for their defense mechanism, their quills.

Western Skinks
tend to live near water in dry, open forests, shrub-steppe, and grassland.

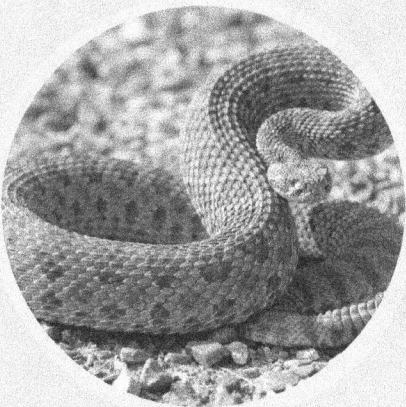

Rattlesnakes
are best identified by their blunt, rattle-tipped tail and thick, stocky bodies.

Gray Foxes
are the only member of the canid that can climb trees.

Common Names
vs.
Scientific Names

A common name of an organism is a name that is based on everyday language. You have heard the common names of plants, animals, and other living things on tv, in books, and at school. Common names can also be referred to as "English" names, popular names, or farmer's names. Common names can vary from place to place. The word for a particular tree may be one thing, but that same tree has a different name in another country. Common names can even vary from region to region, even in the same country.

Scientific names, or Latin names, are given to organisms to make it possible to have uniform names for the same species. Scientific names are in Latin. You may have heard plants or animals referred to by their scientific name or parts of their scientific names. Latin names are also called "binomial nomenclature," which refers to a two-part naming system. The first part of the name - the generic name - refers to the genus to which the species belongs. The second part of the name, the specific name, identifies the species. For example, Tyrannosaurus rex is an example of a widely known scientific name.

Coyote

Canis latrans

COMMON NAME

Elk

Cervus canadensis

LATIN NAME = GENUS + SPECIES

Elk = Cervus canadensis

Coyote = Canis latrans

Find the Match!
Common Names and Latin Names

Match the common name to the scientific name for each animal. The first one is done for you. Use clues on the page before and after this one to complete the matches.

Elk	Haliaeetus leucocephalus
Utah Juniper	Puma concolor
Ponderosa Pine	Eptesicus fuscus
Mountain Lion	Dipodomys ordii
Great Horned Owl	Juniperus osteosperma
Bald Eagle	Hypsiglena chlorophaea
Big Brown Bat	Bubo virginianus
Ord Kangaroo Rat	Cervus canadensis
Desert Night Snake	Pinus ponderosa

Bald Eagle

Haliaeetus leucocephalus

Big Brown Bat
Eptesicus fuscus

Ord Kangaroo Rat
Dipodomys ordii

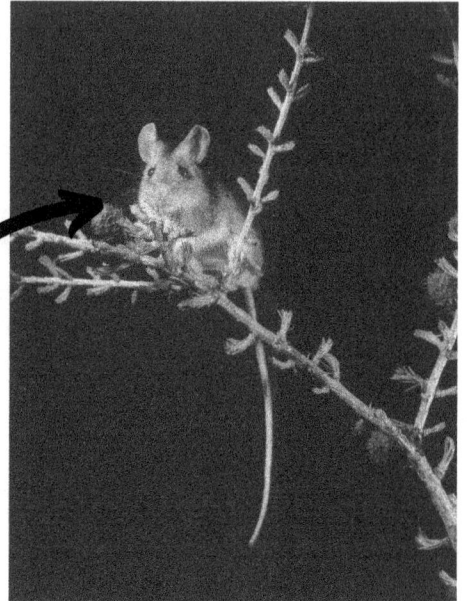

Great Horned Owl
Bubo virginianus

Some plants and animals that live at Great Basin NP

Utah Juniper
Juniperus osteosperma

Mountain Lion
Puma concolor

Desert Night Snake
Hypsiglena chlorophaea

Things To Do Jumble

Unscramble the letters to uncover activities you can do while in Great Basin National Park. Hint: each one ends in -ing.

1. SARTGZA
   ☐☐☐☐☐☐☐☐☐ING

2. IHK
   ☐☐☐ING

3. DBIR
   ☐☐☐☐ING

4. MACP
   ☐☐☐☐ING

5. KINICPC
   ☐☐☐☐☐☐☐ING

6. EISSTEHG
   ☐☐☐☐☐☐☐☐ING

7. VACE LOEPRX
   ☐☐☐☐☐■☐☐☐☐☐☐ING

Word Bank

birding

reading

camping

stargazing

horseback riding

hiking

skiing

singing

cave exploring

sightseeing

picnicking

Making a Difference

It is important to protect the valuable resources of the world, not only beautiful places like national parks.

How many of these things do you do at home? If you answered "no" to more than 10 items, talk to the grownups in your life to see if there are any household habits you might be able to change. Conserving our collective resources helps us all.

Yes	No	Do you...
☐	☐	turn off the water when brushing your teeth?
☐	☐	use LED light bulbs when possible?
☐	☐	use a reusable water bottle instead of disposable ones?
☐	☐	ride your bike or take the bus instead of riding in the car?
☐	☐	have a rain barrel under your roof gutters to collect rain water?
☐	☐	take quick showers?
☐	☐	avoid putting more food on your plate than you will eat?
☐	☐	take reusable lunch containers?
☐	☐	grow a garden?
☐	☐	buy items with less packaging?
☐	☐	recycle paper?
☐	☐	recycle plastic?
☐	☐	have a compost pile at home so you can make your own soil?
☐	☐	pick up trash when you see it on the trail?
☐	☐	plan a "staycation" and fly only when you have to?

_____   _____
of   # of
Yes   No

Add up your score! Are there any "no"s that you want to turn into a yes?

Can you think of any other ways to protect our natural resources?

_____

Helping Bats Thrive

Bats in North America are under threat of a disease called white-nose syndrome. What is this disease? How does it affect bats? What can you do to help?

White-nose syndrome is caused by a fungus called Pseudogymnoascus destructans, or Pd for short. It affects cave-dwelling bats. Unfortunately, this disease is fatal and has killed millions of bats across the United States and Canada. A symptom of this disease is right in the name - a white fuzzy patch on a bat's nose and face. The disease also causes bats to act strangely; they will fly outside in winter when they should be hibernating.

The fungus Pd can be spread from bat to bat, but it can also be spread when bats touch cave surfaces with the fungus. Humans are potential carriers, which is why decontamination is important when visiting the caves at Carlsbad Caverns National Park.

Bats play an important role in our ecosystem. They help control insect populations. Reducing the spread of white-nose syndrome supports bats and their survival.

What can you do to help stop the spread of white-nose syndrome?

Answer: **CLEAN YOUR SHOES, CLOTHES, AND GEAR BEFORE AND AFTER GOING INTO ANY CAVE**

Cipher key:

a	c	d	e	f	g	h	i	n	o	p	r	s	t	u	v
@	1	&	+	*	¿	2	!	^	=	4	?	$	%	5	<

Camping Packing List

What should you take with you when you go camping? Pretend you are in charge of your family camping trip. Make a list of what you would need to be safe and comfortable on an overnight excursion. Some considerations are listed on the side.

1.
2.
3.
4.
5.
6.
7.
8.
9.
10.
11.
12.
13.
14.
15.
16.

- What will you eat at every meal?

- What will the weather be like?

- Where will you sleep?

- What will you do during your free time?

- How luxurious do you want your camp to be?

- How will you cook?

- How will you see at night?

- How will you dispose of trash?

- What might you need in case of emergencies?

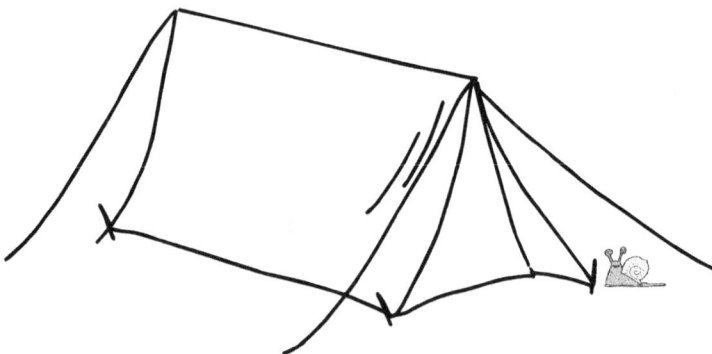

The Ten Essentials

Careful preparation and knowledge are key to a successful adventure into Great Basin's backcountry.

The ten essentials are a list of things that are important to have when you go for longer hikes. If you go on a hike to the <u>backcountry</u>, it is especially important that you have everything you need in case of an emergency. If you get lost or something unforeseen happens, it is good to be prepared to survive until help finds you.

The ten essentials list was developed in the 1930s by an outdoors group called the Mountaineers. Over time and technological advancements, this list has evolved. Can you identify all the things on the current list? Circle each of the "essentials" and cross out everything that doesn't make the cut.

fire: matches, lighter, tinder, and/or stove	a pint of milk	extra money	headlamp, plus extra batteries	extra clothes
extra water	a dog	Polaroid camera	bug net	lightweight games, like a deck of cards
extra food	a roll of duct tape	shelter	sun protection, such as sunglasses, sun-protective clothes, and sunscreen	knife, plus a gear repair kit
a mirror	navigation: map, compass, altimeter, GPS device, or satellite messenger	first aid kit	extra flip-flops	entertainment, such as video games or books

Backcountry - a remote, undeveloped rural area.

Exploring the Dark Sky

Great Basin National Park is a popular destination for stargazing. You may see stars in the night sky here that you may not see at home. Why do you think that is?

For all of time, people from across the world have looked at the night sky and seen images in the stars. They created stories about groups of stars, also called constellations. Create your own constellation you see in the starfield below!

What is your constellation named?

Great Basin Word Search

Words may be horizontal, vertical, diagonal,
or they might even be backwards!

1. wheeler peak
2. bristlecone pine
3. caves
4. bat
5. Nevada
6. wildflowers
7. Fremont
8. limestone
9. pine nuts
10. Stella
11. glacier
12. Teresa
13. sagebrush
14. canyon
15. Lehman
16. camping
17. Ponderosa

```
C W H E E L E R P E A K O W K
H T A S K N L O C H E L A N J
T E P R A L L E T S L B A T B
S M P M G P R S C E B L U C C
W E H D I S A G E B R U S H L
I E L D T C O A D C I E A S I
L I M E S T O N E N S R I C N
D L B A M U I E G N T E K A G
F G L A C I E R B E L D Y D M
L C I C C B O C A V E S O N A
O T A H C H I S O A C E N O N
W A S E R E T I S D O K I Y E
E I O S H U I R E A N A L N W
R C G O N O V E S O E R V A H
S I C E K M I G N I P M A C A
X T N F A E E G L Z I S Q N L
H I D R O F R E M O N T C E E
P P O N D E R O S A E A L A M
```

The Perfect Picnic Spot

Fill in the blanks on this page without looking at the full story. Once you have each line filled out, use the words you've chosen to complete the story on the next page.

EMOTION _

FOOD _

SOMETHING SWEET _

STORE _

MODE OF TRANSPORTATION _

NOUN _

SOMETHING ALIVE _

SAUCE _

PLURAL VEGETABLES _

ADJECTIVE _

PLURAL BODY PART _

ANIMAL _

PLURAL FRUIT _

PLACE _

SOMETHING TALL _

COLOR _

ADJECTIVE _

NOUN _

A DIFFERENT ANIMAL _

FAMILY MEMBER #1 _

FAMILY MEMBER #2 _

VERB THAT ENDS IN -ING _

A DIFFERENT FOOD _

The Perfect Picnic Spot

Use the words from the previous page to complete a silly story.

When my family suggested having our lunch at the Mather Overlook, I was

_ _ _ _ _ _ _ _. I love eating my _ _ _ _ _ _ outside! I knew we had picked up a
EMOTION   FOOD

box of _ _ _ _ _ _ from the _ _ _ _ _ _ _ _ for after lunch, my favorite. We drove up
SOMETHING SWEET   STORE

to the area and I jumped out of the _ _ _ _ _ _ _ _ _. "I will find the perfect spot for
MODE OF TRANSPORTATION

a picnic!" I grabbed a _ _ _ _ _ _ for us to sit on, and I ran off. I passed a picnic
NOUN

table, but it was covered with _ _ _ _ _ _ _ _ so we couldn't sit there. The next
SOMETHING ALIVE

picnic table looked okay, but there were smears of _ _ _ _ _ _ _ and pieces of
SAUCE

_ _ _ _ _ _ _ _ everywhere. The people that were there before must have been
PLURAL VEGETABLES

_ _ _ _ _ _! I gritted my _ _ _ _ _ _ _ together and kept walking down the path,
ADJECTIVE   PLURAL BODY PART

determined to find the perfect spot. I wanted a table with a good view of the

peak. Why was this so hard? If we were lucky, I might even get to see _ _ _ _ _ _
ANIMAL

eating some _ _ _ _ _ _ on the cliffside. They don't have those in _ _ _ _ _ _ _, where
PLURAL FRUIT   PLACE

I am from. I walked down a little hill and there it was, the perfect spot! The

trees towered overhead and looked as tall as _ _ _ _ _ _ _ _. The patch of grass
SOMETHING TALL

was a beautiful _ _ _ _ _ _ _ color. The _ _ _ _ _ _ flowers were growing on
COLOR   ADJECTIVE

the side of a _ _ _ _ _ _ _. I looked across the overlooks edge and even saw a
NOUN

_ _ _ _ _ _ _ _ _ on the edge of a rock. I looked back to see my _ _ _ _ _ _ _ _ _ and
DIFFERENT ANIMAL   FAMILY MEMBER #1

_ _ _ _ _ _ _ _ _ _ _ _ _ _ _ _ _ _ a picnic basket. "I hope you brought plenty of
FAMILY MEMBER #2   VERB THAT ENDS IN ING

_ _ _ _ _ _ _ _, I'm starving!"
A DIFFERENT FOOD

27

Reducing Your Footprint

Your carbon "footprint" is the amount of carbon dioxide released into the air because of your own energy needs. All people have basic needs like transportation, electricity, food, clothing, and other goods. Governments and private businesses have the biggest impact on the environment, but our individual choices can impact the planet too.

In the box below, make a footprint. You can use your own foot and trace it, step in paint and make a footprint, or draw a footprint freehand.

How does your community try to reduce its carbon footprint? You can use examples from your town, your school, or your family. See page 20 for ideas.

Wildlife Wisdom

The national park is home to many different kinds of animals. Seeing wildlife can be an exciting part of visiting the national park but it is important to remember that these animals are wild. They need plenty of space and a healthy habitat where they can find their own food. Part of this is not allowing animals to eat any human food. This is their home and we are the visitors. We need to be respectful of the wildlife in the park.

Directions: Circle the highlighted words that best complete the following sentences.

If an animal changes its behavior because of your presence, you are:
   A) too close
   B) funny looking
   C) dehydrated and should drink more water

The best thing we can do to help wild animals survive is:
   A) make them pets
   B) protect their habitat
   C) knit them winter sweaters

In a national park, it is okay to share your food with wild animals:
   A) never
   B) always
   C) sometimes

When you're hiking in an area where there are bears, you should warn bears that you are entering their space by:
   A) hiking quietly
   B) making noise
   C) wearing bright colors

At night, park rangers care for the animals by:
   A) putting them back into their cages
   B) tucking them into bed
   C) leaving them alone

If you see an abandoned bird's nest, it is best to:
   A) pet the baby birds
   B) leave it alone
   C) crunch the empty eggshells

Bears look under logs in hopes of finding:
   A) granola bars
   B) insects
   C) peanuts to eat

The place where an animal lives is called its:
   A) condo
   B) habitat
   C) crib

29

Hike to a Lake

start here

Lehman Caves Word Search

The Lehman Caves await your exploration! Year round, visitors to Great Basin National Park can reserve a ranger-led tour through the Lehman Caves, where Park Rangers explain the history, ecology, and geology of the caves.

1. marble
2. bedrock
3. carbonic
4. passageway
5. room
6. formation
7. column
8. geologic
9. soda straw
10. dark
11. woodrat
12. flashlight
13. helmet
14. explore
15. ranger
16. lodge room
17. gothic palace
18. grand palace
19. queens bath

```
P A S S A G E W A Y I D E O G
H A D A F O R M A T I O N R O
T V D T E M L E H W A L K O T
S E U D S P E G C Y U T B M H
G E O L O G I C L E Y R S K I
M P D L Y L R A C N M U L O C
C O S E H R C R O O M R L E P
A R B S M K I B D I L T E X A
L S A O G I L O E O U D C P L
L L I D A R K N K E U G A L A
F S A A A T I I N L K B L O C
S H N S K A O C S A S K A R E
T J O T F H I N Z I I L P E C
E T A R D O O W K C O R D E B
R W R A N G E R D O A O N E M
T T E W G R E E E L B R A M T
L O D G E R O O M O A P R E B
Q U E E N S B A T H Y S G O N
```

Leave No Trace Quiz

Leave No Trace is a concept that helps people make decisions during outdoor recreation that protects the environment. There are seven principles that guide us when we spend time outdoors, whether you are in a national park or not. Are you an expert in Leave No Trace? Take this quiz and find out!

1. How can you plan ahead and prepare to ensure you have the best experience you can in the national park?
   a. Make sure you stop by the ranger station for a map and to ask about current conditions.
   b. Just wing it! You will know the best trail when you see it.
   c. Stick to your plan, even if conditions change. You traveled a long way to get here, and you should stick to your plan.
2. What is an example of traveling on a durable surface?
   a. Walking only on the designated path.
   b. Walking on the grass that borders the trail if the trail is very muddy.
   c. Taking a shortcut if you can find one because it means you will be walking less.
3. Why should you dispose of waste properly?
   a. You don't need to. Park rangers love to pick up the trash you leave behind.
   b. You should actually leave your leftovers behind, because animals will eat them. It is important to make sure they aren't hungry.
   c. So that other peoples' experiences of the park are not impacted by you leaving your waste behind.
4. How can you best follow the concept "leave what you find?"
   a. Take only a small rock or leaf to remember your trip.
   b. Take pictures, but leave any physical items where they are.
   c. Leave everything you find, unless it may be rare like an arrowhead, then it is okay to take.
5. What is not a good example of minimizing campfire impacts?
   a. Only having a campfire in a pre-existing campfire ring.
   b. Checking in with current conditions when you consider making a campfire.
   c. Building a new campfire ring in a location that has a better view.
6. What is a poor example of respecting wildlife?
   a. Building squirrel houses out of rocks so the squirrels have a place to live.
   b. Stay far away from wildlife and give them plenty of space.
   c. Reminding your grown-ups not to drive too fast in animal habitats while visiting the park.
7. How can you show consideration of other visitors?
   a. Play music on your speaker so other people at the campground can enjoy it.
   b. Wear headphones on the trail if you choose to listen to music.
   c. Make sure to yell "Hello!" to every animal you see at top volume.

Park Poetry

America's parks inspire art of all kinds. Painters, sculptors, photographers, writers, and artists of all mediums have taken inspiration from natural beauty. They have turned their inspiration into great works.

Use this space to write your own poem about the park. Think about what you have experienced or seen. Use descriptive language to create an acrostic poem. This type of poem has the first letter of each line spell out another word. Create an acrostic that spells out the word "Basin."

B _____

A _____

S _____

I _____

N _____

Below mountains

Across desert floor

Slithering snakes

Inconspicuous in the

Nighttime air

Big brown bats

Across the

Sky

Into the

Night

Bristlecone General Store

After hours on the road, you finally make it to Baker, Nevada. You are so close to finally stepping into the park when you realize your backpack is missing. Oh no! All your supplies are gone! You need to hit the general store in town and restock before your adventure.

The letters of several key adventure items are all jumbled up. Can you unscramble the words and figure out what you need?

WEART

ENSECRSUN

MOSSPAC

NCSASK

KETACJ

CHULN

PAM

Now arrange the circled letters to figure out another name for US Route 50.

O H O   O O N L I S O   R O O D

I N   A O E R I O A

Catch a Fish at Baker Creek

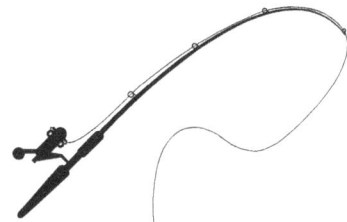

start here

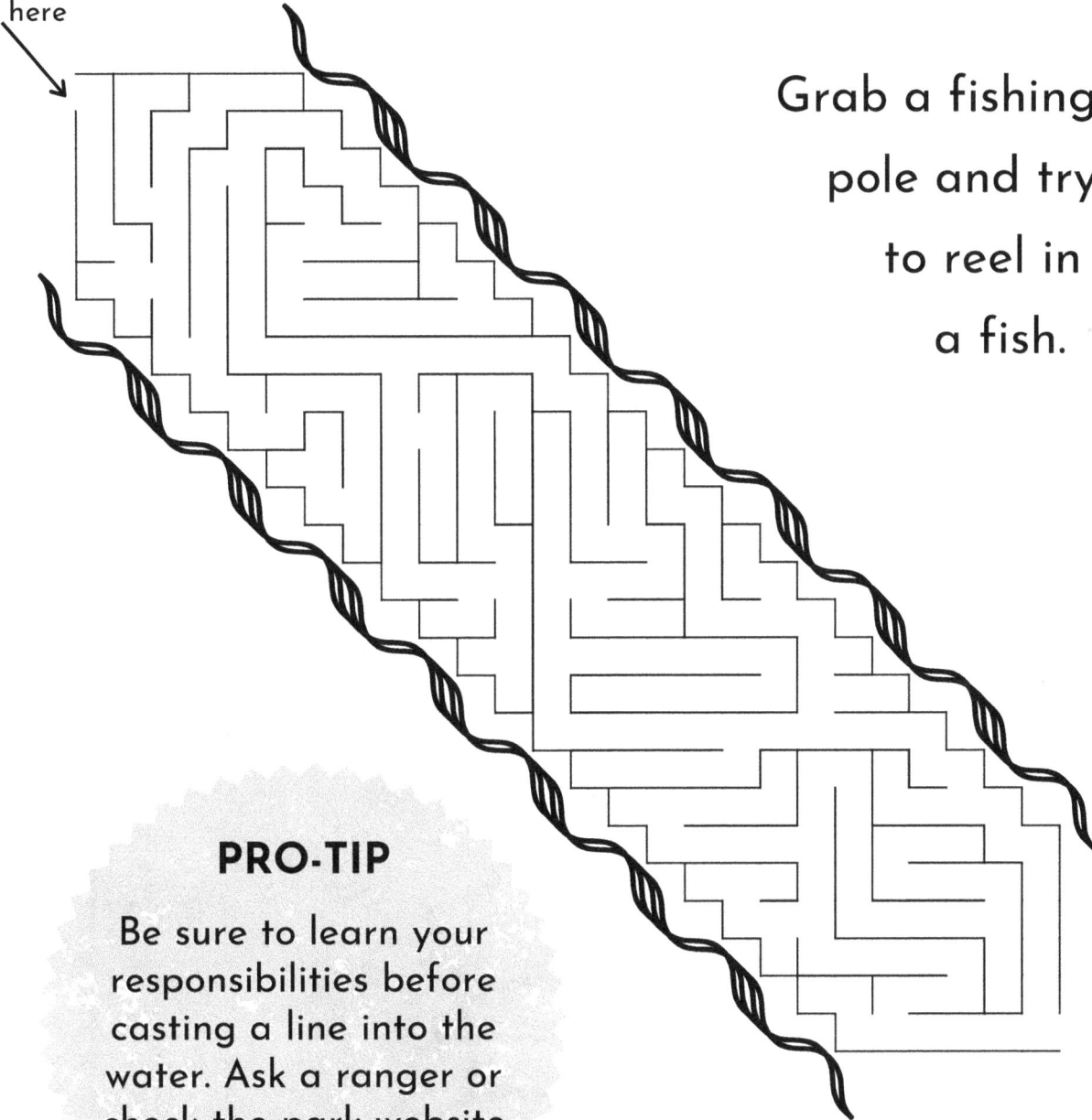

Grab a fishing pole and try to reel in a fish.

PRO-TIP

Be sure to learn your responsibilities before casting a line into the water. Ask a ranger or check the park website before you go.

Stacking Rocks

Have you ever seen stacks of rocks while hiking in national parks? Do you know what they are or what they mean? These rock piles are called cairns and often mark hiking routes in parks. Every park has a different way to maintain trails and cairns. However, they all have the same rule: If you come across a cairn, do not disturb it!

Color the cairn and the rules to remember.

1. Do not tamper with cairns.

If a cairn is tampered with or an unauthorized one is built, then future visitors may become disoriented or even lost.

2. Do not build unauthorized cairns.

Moving rocks disturbs the soil and makes the area more prone to erosion. Disturbing rocks can disturb fragile plants.

3. Do not add to existing cairns.

Authorized cairns are carefully designed. Adding to them can actually cause them to collapse.

Decoding Using American Sign Language

American Sign Language, also called ASL for short, is a language that many Deaf people or people who are hard of hearing use to communicate. People use ASL to communicate with their hands. Did you know people from all over the country and world travel to national parks? You may hear people speaking other languages. You might also see people using ASL. Use the American Manual Alphabet chart to decode some national parks facts.

This was the first national park to be established:

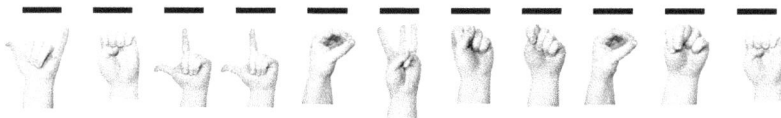

_ _ _ _ _ _ _ _ _ _

This is the biggest national park in the US:

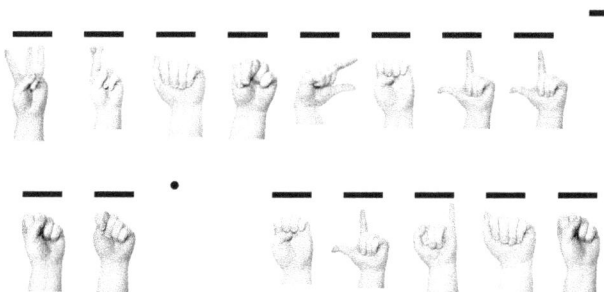

_ _ _ _ _ _ _ -

_ _ . _ _ _ _

This is the most visited national park:

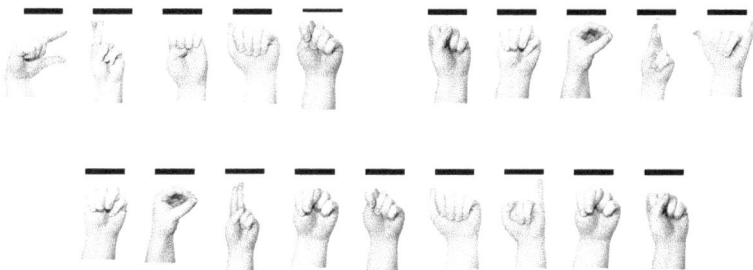

_ _ _ _ _ _ _ _ _

_ _ _ _ _ _ _

Aa	Bb	Cc	Dd	Ee
Ff	Gg		Hh	Ii
Jj	Kk	Ll	Mm	Nn
Oo	Pp		Qq	Rr
Ss	Tt		Uu	Vv
Ww	Xx		Yy	Zz

Hint: Pay close attention to the position of the thumb!

Try it! Using the chart, try to make the letters of the alphabet with your hand. What is the hardest letter to make? Can you spell out your name? Show a friend or family member and have them watch you spell out the name of the national park you are in.

Go Birdwatching at Wheeler Peak Campground

start here

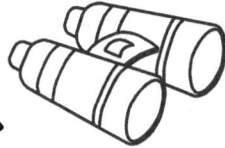

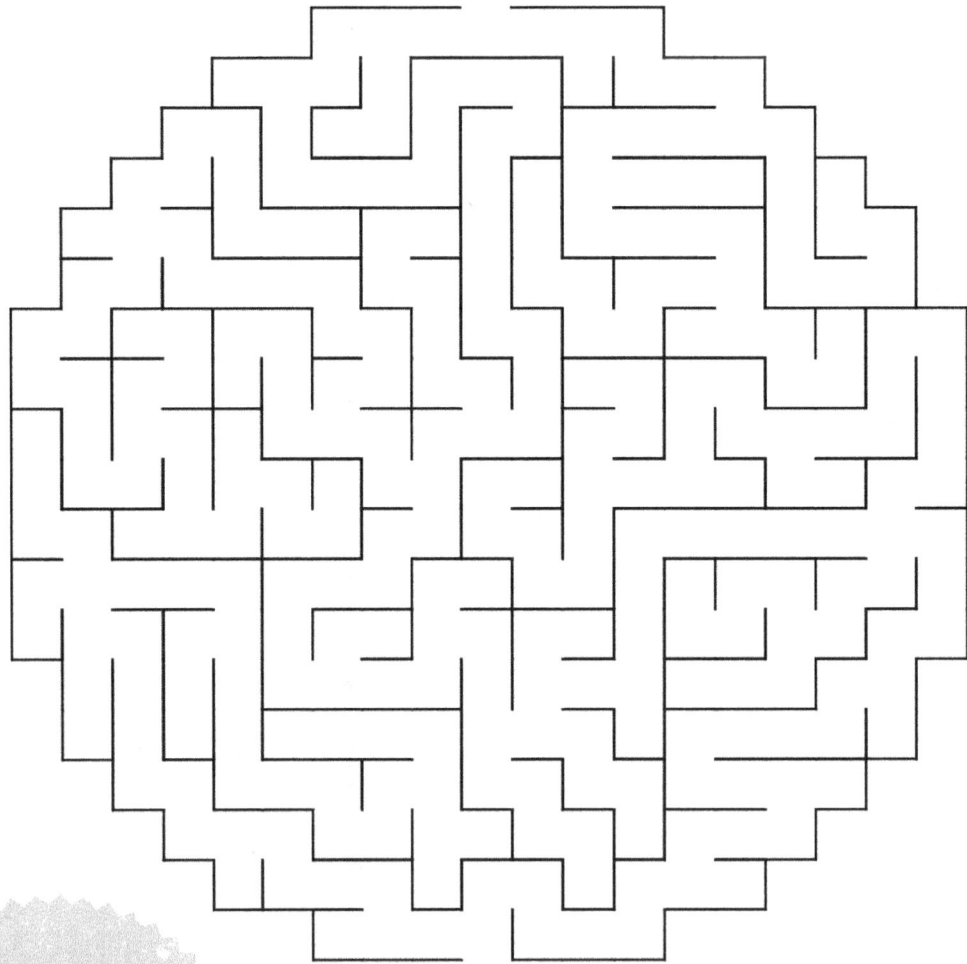

DID YOU KNOW?
Great Basin NP is home to several birds of prey, including eagles, hawks, and owls. Birds of prey are birds that hunt other animals for food.

Butterflies of Great Basin

Dozens of species of butterflies and moths live in Great Basin National Park. Their wingspan size varies, as do the patterns on their wings. Design your own butterfly below. Make sure the wings are symmetrical, which means both sides match.

A Hike at Bristlecone Grove

Fill in the blanks on this page without looking at the full story. Once you have each line filled out, use the words you've chosen to complete the story on the next page.

ADJECTIVE _____

SOMETHING TO EAT _____

SOMETHING TO DRINK _____

NOUN _____

ARTICLE OF CLOTHING _____

BODY PART _____

VERB _____

ANIMAL _____

SAME TYPE OF FOOD _____

ADJECTIVE _____

SAME ANIMAL _____

VERB THAT ENDS IN "ED" _____

NUMBER _____

A DIFFERENT NUMBER _____

SOMETHING THAT FLIES _____

LIGHT SOURCE _____

PLURAL NOUN _____

FAMILY MEMBER _____

YOUR NICKNAME _____

A Hike at Bristlecone Grove

Use the words from the previous page to complete a silly story.

I went for a hike at Bristlecone Grove today. In my favorite _____
ADJECTIVE

backpack, I made sure to pack a map so I wouldn't get lost. I also threw in an

extra _____ just in case I got hungry and a bottle of _____.
SOMETHING TO EAT   SOMETHING TO DRINK

I put on my _____ spray, and I tied a _____ around my
NOUN   ARTICLE OF CLOTHING

_____, in case it gets chilly. I started to _____ down the path. As
BODY PART   VERB

soon as I turned the corner, I came face to face with a(n) _____. I think
ANIMAL

it was as startled as I was! What should I do? I had to think fast! Should I

give it some of my _____? No. I had to remember what the
SAME TYPE OF FOOD

_____ ranger told me: "If you see one, back away slowly and try not to
ADJECTIVE

scare it." Soon enough, the _____ _____ away. The coast
SAME ANIMAL   VERB THAT ENDS IN ED

was clear. _____ hours later, I finally reached the lookout. I felt like I could
NUMBER

see for a _____ miles. I took a picture of a _____ so I could always
A DIFFERENT NUMBER   NOUN

remember this moment. As I was putting my camera away, a _____
SOMETHING THAT FLIES

flew by, reminding me that it was almost nighttime. I turned on my

_____ and headed back. I could hear the _____ singing their
LIGHT SOURCE   PLURAL INSECT

evening song. Just as I was getting tired, I saw my _____ and our tent.
FAMILY MEMBER

"Welcome back _____! How was your hike?"
NICKNAME

Snail Mail

Design a postcard to send to a friend or a family member. Who do you want to tell about Great Basin National Park? In the first template, write your message. In the second template, create a design for the front of the postcard. You could show something you saw, something you did, or something you want to do in the national park.

Postcard

Let's Go Camping at Baker Creek

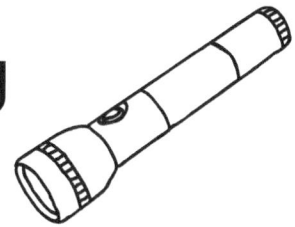

Words may be horizontal, vertical, diagonal, or they might even be backwards!

1. tent
2. camp stove
3. sleeping bag
4. bug spray
5. sunscreen
6. map
7. flashlight
8. pillow
9. lantern
10. ice
11. snacks
12. smores
13. water
14. first aid kit
15. chair
16. cards
17. books
18. games
19. trail
20. hat

```
D P P I L L O W D B T E A C I
E O A D P R E A A M B R C A N
P W C A M P S T O V E I H X G
R A H S G E L E B E E D A P S
E L B U G S P R A Y N G I E A
S I A H G C I C N N M E R C N
C W N L A F I R S K O O B F K
M T A E M I L E L H M R W L J
T A P R E A O R E S L B A A B
S M P A S R R T E N T L U S C
C E A I I R C G P E I U J H A
S S N A C K S S I M O K I L R
I J R S F O I S N J R A Q I D
C Y E T L E V E G U O R V G S
E W T A K C A B B S S O H H M
X J N F I R S T A I D K I T T
U A A E S S E N G E T P V A B
C J L I A R T D N A M A H A S
```

43

All in the Day of a Park Ranger

Park Rangers are hardworking individuals dedicated to protecting our parks, monuments, museums, and more. They take care of the natural and cultural resources for future generations. Rangers also help protect the visitors of the park. Their responsibilities are broad and they work both with the public and behind the scenes.

What have you seen park rangers do? Use your knowledge of the duties of park rangers to fill out a typical daily schedule, listing one activity for each hour. Feel free to make up your own, but some examples of activities are provided on the right. Read carefully! Not all the example activities are befitting a ranger.

Time	Activity
6 am	Lead a sunrise hike
7 am	
8 am	
9 am	
10 am	
11 am	
12 pm	Enjoy a lunch break outside
1 pm	
2 pm	
3 pm	
4 pm	Teach visitors about the geology of the Snake Range
5 pm	
6 pm	
7 pm	
8 pm	
9 pm	

- feed the migratory birds
- build trails for visitors to enjoy
- throw rocks off the side of the mountain
- rescue lost hikers
- study animal behavior
- record air quality data
- answer questions at the visitor center
- pick wildflowers
- pick up litter
- share marshmallows with squirrels
- repair handrails
- lead a class on a field trip
- catch frogs or toads and make them race
- lead people on educational hikes
- write articles for the park website
- protect the river from pollution
- remove non-native plants from the park
- study how climate change is affecting the park
- give a talk about mountain lions
- lead a program for campers on bats.

If you were a park ranger, which of the above tasks would you enjoy most?

_____

Draw Yourself as a Park Ranger

RANGER

What are Reptiles?

Reptiles are a group of animals that are cold-blooded, have scales, breathe air, and usually lay eggs. Label each reptile using the word bank below.

1. _____

2. _____

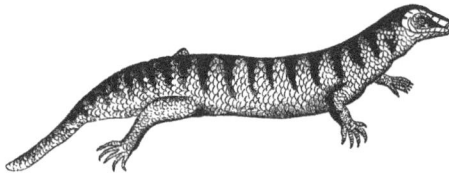

3. _____

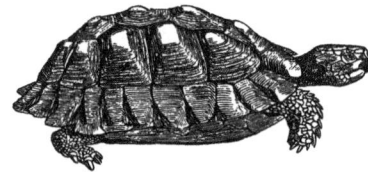

4. _____

WORD BANK

Tortoise	Frog
Toad	Lizard
Snake	Skink
Salamander	Crocodile

DID YOU KNOW?
Not all of the reptiles on this page live in Great Basin National Park, but several species of snakes and lizards like to call the Great Basin home.

What reptiles have you seen in Great Basin National Park? If you haven't seen any, what do you want to see? Write or draw your answer in the box below.

Sound Exploration

Spend a minute or two listening to all of the sounds around you.
Draw your favorite sound.

How did this sound make you feel?

_____

_____

What did you think when you heard this sound?

_____

_____

Draw a Fox

Complete the picture below by drawing the other half of the fox. Complete the image by coloring it in.

Great Basin National Park is home to kit foxes, gray foxes, and likely red foxes. These animals are among the region's carnivores alongside other predators such as coyotes, mountain lions, and bobcats.

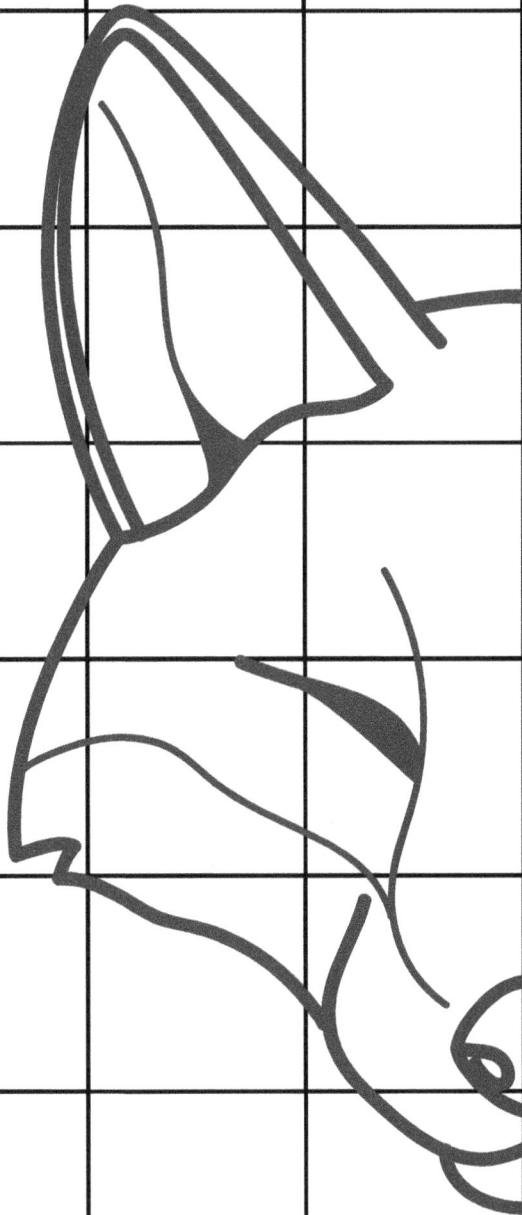

63 National Parks

How many other national parks have you been to? Which one do you want to visit next? Note that if some of these parks fall on the border of more than one state, you may check it off more than once!

Alaska
- [ ] Denali National Park
- [ ] Gates of the Arctic National Park
- [ ] Glacier Bay National Park
- [ ] Katmai National Park
- [ ] Kenai Fjords National Park
- [ ] Kobuk Valley National Park
- [ ] Lake Clark National Park
- [ ] Wrangell-St. Elias National Park

American Samoa
- [ ] National Park of American Samoa

Arizona
- [ ] Grand Canyon National Park
- [ ] Petrified Forest National Park
- [ ] Saguaro National Park

Arkansas
- [ ] Hot Springs National Park

California
- [ ] Channel Islands National Park
- [ ] Death Valley National Park
- [ ] Joshua Tree National Park
- [ ] Kings Canyon National Park
- [ ] Lassen Volcanic National Park
- [ ] Pinnacles National Park
- [ ] Redwood National Park
- [ ] Sequoia National Park
- [ ] Yosemite National Park

Colorado
- [ ] Black Canyon of the Gunnison National Park
- [ ] Great Sand Dunes National Park
- [ ] Mesa Verde National Park
- [ ] Rocky Mountain National Park

Florida
- [ ] Biscayne National Park
- [ ] Dry Tortugas National Park
- [ ] Everglades National Park

Hawaii
- [ ] Haleakalā National Park
- [ ] Hawai'i Volcanoes National Park

Idaho
- [ ] Yellowstone National Park

Kentucky
- [ ] Mammoth Cave National Park

Indiana
- [ ] Indiana Dunes National Park

Maine
- [ ] Acadia National Park

Michigan
- [ ] Isle Royale National Park

Minnesota
- [ ] Voyageurs National Park

Missouri
- [ ] Gateway Arch National Park

Montana
- [ ] Glacier National Park
- [ ] Yellowstone National Park

Nevada
- [ ] Death Valley National Park
- [ ] Great Basin National Park

New Mexico
- [ ] Carlsbad Caverns National Park
- [ ] White Sands National Park

North Dakota
- [ ] Theodore Roosevelt National Park

North Carolina
- [ ] Great Smoky Mountains National Park

Ohio
- [ ] Cuyahoga Valley National Park

Oregon
- [ ] Crater Lake National Park

South Carolina
- [ ] Congaree National Park

South Dakota
- [ ] Badlands National Park
- [ ] Wind Cave National Park

Tennessee
- [ ] Great Smoky Mountains National Park

Texas
- [ ] Big Bend National Park
- [ ] Guadalupe Mountains National Park

Utah
- [ ] Arches National Park
- [ ] Bryce Canyon National Park
- [ ] Canyonlands National Park
- [ ] Capitol Reef National Park
- [ ] Zion National Park

Virgin Islands
- [ ] Virgin Islands National Park

Virginia
- [ ] Shenandoah National Park

Washington
- [ ] Mount Rainier National Park
- [ ] North Cascades National Park
- [ ] Olympic National Park

West Virginia
- [ ] New River Gorge National Park

Wyoming
- [ ] Grand Teton National Park
- [ ] Yellowstone National Park

Other National Parks Crossword

Besides Great Basin National Park, there are 62 other diverse and beautiful national parks across the United States. Try your hand at this crossword. If you need help, look at the previous page for some hints.

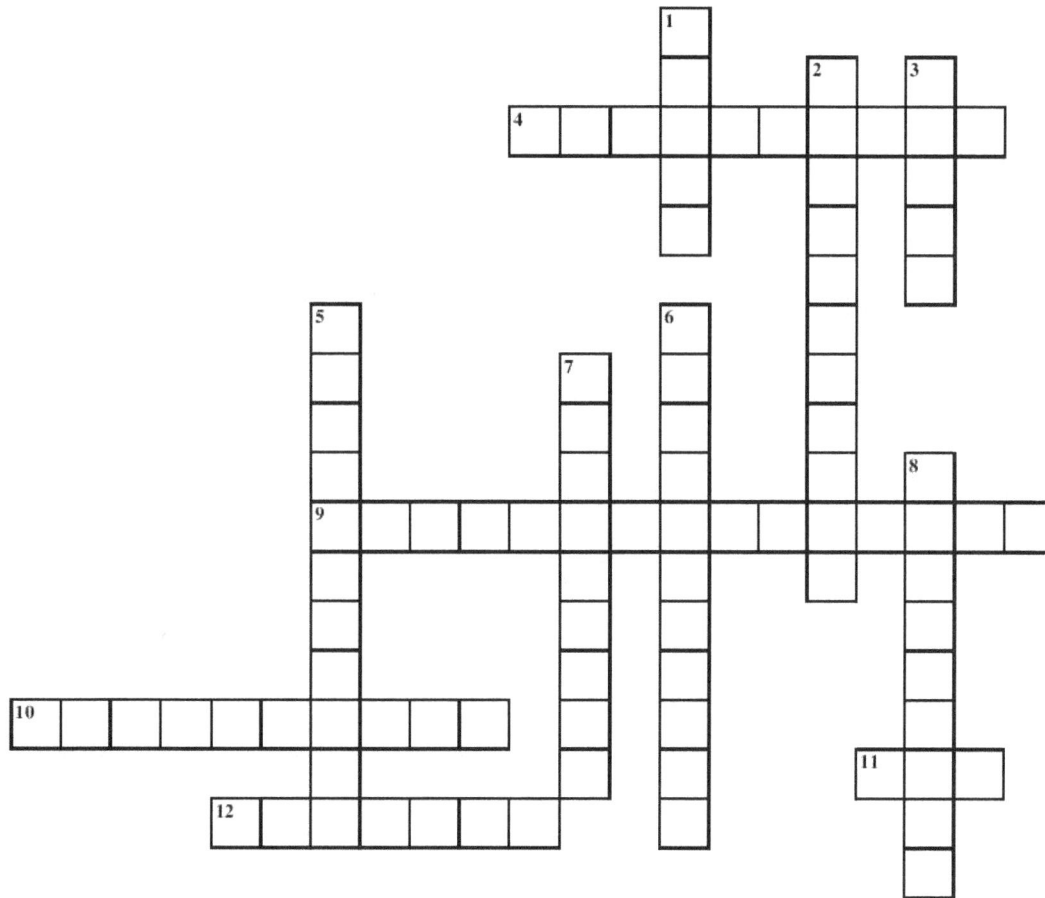

Down

1. State where Acadia National Park is located
2. This national park has the Spanish word for turtle in it
3. Number of national parks in Alaska
5. This national park has some of the hottest temperatures in the world
6. This national park is the only one in Idaho
7. This toothsome creature can famously be found in Everglades National Park
8. Only president with a national park named for them

Across

4. This state has the most national parks
9. This park has some of the newest land in the US, caused by volcanic eruptions
10. This park has the deepest lake in the United States
11. This color shows up in the name of a national park in California
12. This national park deserves a gold medal

Which National Park Will You Go To Next?
Word Search

1. Zion
2. Big Bend
3. Glacier
4. Olympic
5. Sequoia
6. Bryce
7. Mesa Verde
8. Biscayne
9. Wind Cave
10. Great Basin
11. Katmai
12. Yellowstone
13. Voyageurs
14. Arches
15. Badlands
16. Denali
17. Glacier Bay
18. Hot Springs

```
F  M  M  E  S  A  V  E  R  D  E  B  N  E  Y
E  A  B  I  G  B  E  N  D  E  S  A  S  E  M
Y  L  I  C  A  L  O  Y  N  E  E  D  L  T  G
D  M  G  A  S  S  A  U  C  N  R  L  U  E  R
C  E  L  I  I  T  S  C  R  E  O  A  A  K  E
S  N  A  W  Y  E  E  O  I  W  T  N  A  C  A
G  I  C  H  A  A  Q  C  S  E  M  D  N  S  T
N  O  I  Z  P  R  U  T  I  M  R  S  N  E  B
I  W  E  L  M  P  O  N  B  W  E  B  K  H  A
R  J  R  F  D  N  I  F  L  I  H  B  U  C  S
P  A  B  E  E  S  A  N  E  S  O  P  W  R  I
S  J  A  E  N  Y  A  C  S  I  B  A  U  A  N
T  C  Y  I  A  D  O  H  H  Y  M  E  A  L  R
O  T  A  T  L  M  L  E  S  E  G  R  W  R  J
H  S  T  O  I  K  A  T  M  A  I  R  O  P  B
I  C  H  U  R  C  O  L  Y  M  P  I  C  O  U
O  Y  G  T  S  D  E  O  S  B  R  Y  C  E  T
W  I  N  D  C  A  V  E  I  N  R  O  H  E  M
```

52

Field Notes

Spend some time reflecting on your trip to Great Basin National Park. Your field notes will help you remember the things you experienced. Use the space below to write about your day.

While I was at Great Basin National Park...

I saw:

_____

_____

_____

_____

_____

I heard:

_____

_____

_____

_____

I felt:

_____

_____

Draw a picture of your
favorite thing in the park.

I wondered:

_____

_____

_____

_____

_____

ANSWER KEY

Go Horseback Riding on the Bristlecone Grove

Help find the horse's lost shoe!

start here →

DID YOU KNOW?

Horseback riding is a popular activity in Great Basin National Park. There are many trails you can take horses for day or overnight trips.

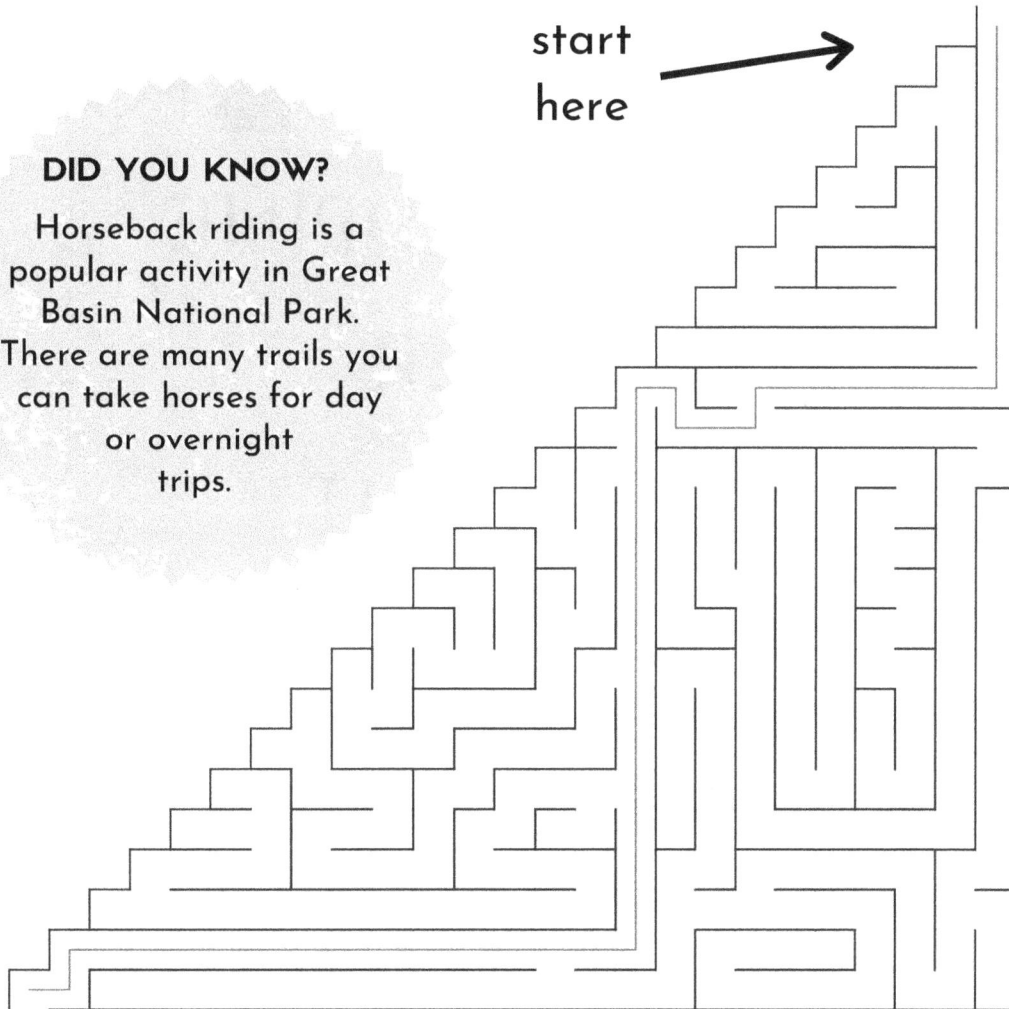

Answers: Who lives here?

Below are 10 plants and animals that live in the park.
Use the word bank to fill in the clues below.

WORD BANK: PORCUPINE, PYGMY RABBIT, HOARY BAT, BIGHORN SHEEP, WESTERN SKINK, RINGTAIL, MALLARD, RATTLESNAKE, KILLDEER, GRAY FOX

GRAY ■ FOX
PO R CUPINE
KILLD E ER
PYGMY ■ R A BBIT
RAT T LESNAKE
HOARY ■ B AT
M A LLARD
BIGHORN ■ S HEEP
R I NGTAIL
WESTER N ■ SKINK

Find the Match!
Common Names and Latin Names

Match the common name to the scientific name for each animal. The first one is done for you. Use clues on the page before and after this one to complete the matches.

Common Name	Scientific Name
Elk	Haliaeetus leucocephalus
Utah Juniper	Puma concolor
Ponderosa Pine	Eptesicus fuscus
Mountain Lion	Dipodomys ordii
Great Horned Owl	Juniperus osteosperma
Bald Eagle	Hypsiglena chlorophaea
Big Brown Bat	Bubo virginianus
Ord Kangaroo Rat	Cervus canadensis
Desert Night Snake	Pinus ponderosa

Bald Eagle

Haliaeetus leucocephalus

Helping Bats Thrive

What can you do to help stop the spread of white-nose syndrome?

clean your shoes, clothes, and gear before
and after going into any cave.

Jumbles Answers

1. STARGAZING

2. BIRDING

3. CAMPING

4. PICNICKING

5. SIGHTSEEING

6. CAVE EXPLORING

National Park Emblem Answers

1. This represents all plants: **Sequoia Tree**

2. This represents all animals: **Bison**

3. This represents the landscapes: **Mountains**

4. This represents the waters protected by the park service: **Water**

5. This represents the historical and archeological values: **Arrowhead**

Answers: The Ten Essentials

Careful preparation and knowledge are key to a successful adventure into Great Basin's backcountry.

The ten essentials are a list of things that are important to have when you go for longer hikes. If you go on a hike to the <u>backcountry</u>, it is especially important that you have everything you need in case of an emergency. If you get lost or something unforeseen happens, it is good to be prepared to survive until help finds you.

The ten essentials list was developed in the 1930s by an outdoors group called the Mountaineers. Over time and technological advancements, this list has evolved. Can you identify all the things on the current list? Circle each of the "essentials" and cross out everything that doesn't make the cut.

(fire: matches, lighter, tinder, and/or stove)	~~a pair of milk~~	~~extra money~~	(headlamp, plus extra batteries)	(extra clothes)
(extra water)	~~a dog~~	~~Polaroid camera~~	~~bug net~~	~~lightweight games like a deck of cards~~
(extra food)	~~a roll of duct tape~~	(shelter)	(sun protection, such as sunglasses, sun-protective clothes, and sunscreen)	(knife, plus a gear repair kit)
~~a mirror~~	(navigation: map, compass, altimeter, GPS device, or satellite messenger)	(first aid kit)	~~extra flip-flops~~	~~entertainment like video games or books~~

Backcountry - a remote undeveloped rural area.

Great Basin Word Search

Words may be horizontal, vertical, diagonal,
or they might even be backwards!

1. wheeler peak
2. bristlecone pine
3. caves
4. bat
5. Nevada
6. wildflowers
7. Fremont
8. limestone
9. pine nuts
10. Stella
11. glacier
12. Teresa
13. sagebrush
14. canyon
15. Lehman
16. camping
17. Ponderosa

```
C W H E E L E R P E A K O W K
H T A S K N L O C H E L A N J
T E P R A L L E T S L B A T B
S M P M G P R S C E B L U C C
W E H D I S A G E B R U S H L
I E L D T C O A D C I E A S I
L I M E S T O N E N S R I C N
D L B A M U I E G N T E K A G
F G L A C I E R B E L D Y D M
L C I C C B O C A V E S O N A
O T A H C H I S O A C E N O N
W A S E R E T I S D O K I Y E
E I O S H U I R E A N A L N W
R C G O N O V E S O E R V A H
S I C E K M I G N I P M A C A
X T N F A E E G L Z I S Q N L
H I D R O F R E M O N T C E E
P P O N D E R O S A E A L A M
```

60

Wildlife Wisdom

The national park is home to many different kinds of animals. Seeing wildlife can be an exciting part of visiting the national park but it is important to remember that these animals are wild. They need plenty of space and a healthy habitat where they can find their own food. Part of this is not allowing animals to eat any human food. This is their home and we are the visitors. We need to be respectful of the wildlife in the park.

Directions: Circle the highlighted words that best complete the following sentences.

If an animal changes its behavior because of your presence, you are:
A) too close
B) funny looking
C) dehydrated and should drink more water

The best thing we can do to help wild animals survive is:
A) make them pets
B) protect their habitat
C) knit them winter sweaters

In a national park, it is okay to share your food with wild animals:
A) never
B) always
C) sometimes

When you're hiking in an area where there are bears, you should warn bears that you are entering their space by:
A) hiking quietly
B) making noise
C) wearing bright colors

At night, park rangers care for the animals by:
A) putting them back into their cages
B) tucking them into bed
C) leaving them alone

If you see an abandoned bird's nest, it is best to:
A) pet the baby birds
B) leave it alone
C) crunch the empty eggshells

Bears look under logs in hopes of finding:
A) granola bars
B) insects
C) peanuts to eat

The place where an animal lives is called its:
A) condo
B) habitat
C) crib

Solution: Hike to a Lake

Lehman Caves Word Search

The Lehman Caves await your exploration! Year round, visitors to Great Basin National park can reserve a ranger-led tour through the Lehman Caves, where Park Rangers explain the history, ecology and geology of the caves.

1. marble
2. bedrock
3. carbonic
4. passageway
5. room
6. formation
7. column
8. geologic
9. soda straw
10. dark
11. woodrat
12. flashlight
13. helmet
14. explore
15. ranger
16. lodge room
17. gothic palace
18. grand palace
19. queens bath

```
P A S S A G E W A Y I D E O G
H A D A F O R M A T I O N R O
T V D T E M L E H W A L K O T
S E U D S P E G C Y U T B M H
G E O L O G I C L E Y R S K I
M P D L Y L R A C N M U L O C
C O S E H R C R O O M R L E P
A R B S M K I B D I L T E X A
L S A O G I L O E O U D C P L
L L I D A R K N K E U G A L A
F S A A A T I N L K B L O C
S H N S K A O C S A S K A R E
T J O T F H I N Z I I L P E C
E T A R D O O W K C O R D E B
R W R A N G E R D O A O N E M
T T E W G R E E E L B R A M T
L O D G E R O O M O A P R E B
Q U E E N S B A T H Y S G O N
```

63

Answers: Leave No Trace Quiz

1. How can you plan ahead and prepare to ensure you have the best experience you can in the National Park?

    A. Make sure you stop by the ranger station for a map and to ask about current conditions.

2. What is an example of traveling on a durable surface?

    A. Walking only on the designated path.

3. Why should you dispose of waste properly?

    C. So that other peoples' experiences of the park are not impacted by you leaving your waste behind.

4. How can you best follow the concept "leave what you find?"

    B. Take pictures but leave any physical items where they are.

5. What is not a good example of minimizing campfire impacts?

    C. Building a new campfire ring in a location that has a better view.

6. What is a poor example of respecting wildlife?

    A. Building squirrel houses out of rocks from the river so the squirrels have a place to live.

7. How can you show consideration of other visitors?

    B. Wear headphones on the trail if you choose to listen to music.

Bristlecone General Store

WEART	ENSECRSUN
W A T E R	S U N S C R E E N

MOSSPAC	NCSASK
C O M P A S S	S N A C K S

KETACJ	CHULN	PAM
J A C K E T	L U N C H	M A P

Now arrange the circled letters to figure out another name for US Route 50.

T H E   L O N L I E S T   R O A D

I N   A M E R I C A

64

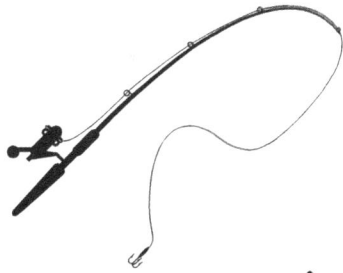

Solution: Catch a Fish at Baker Creek

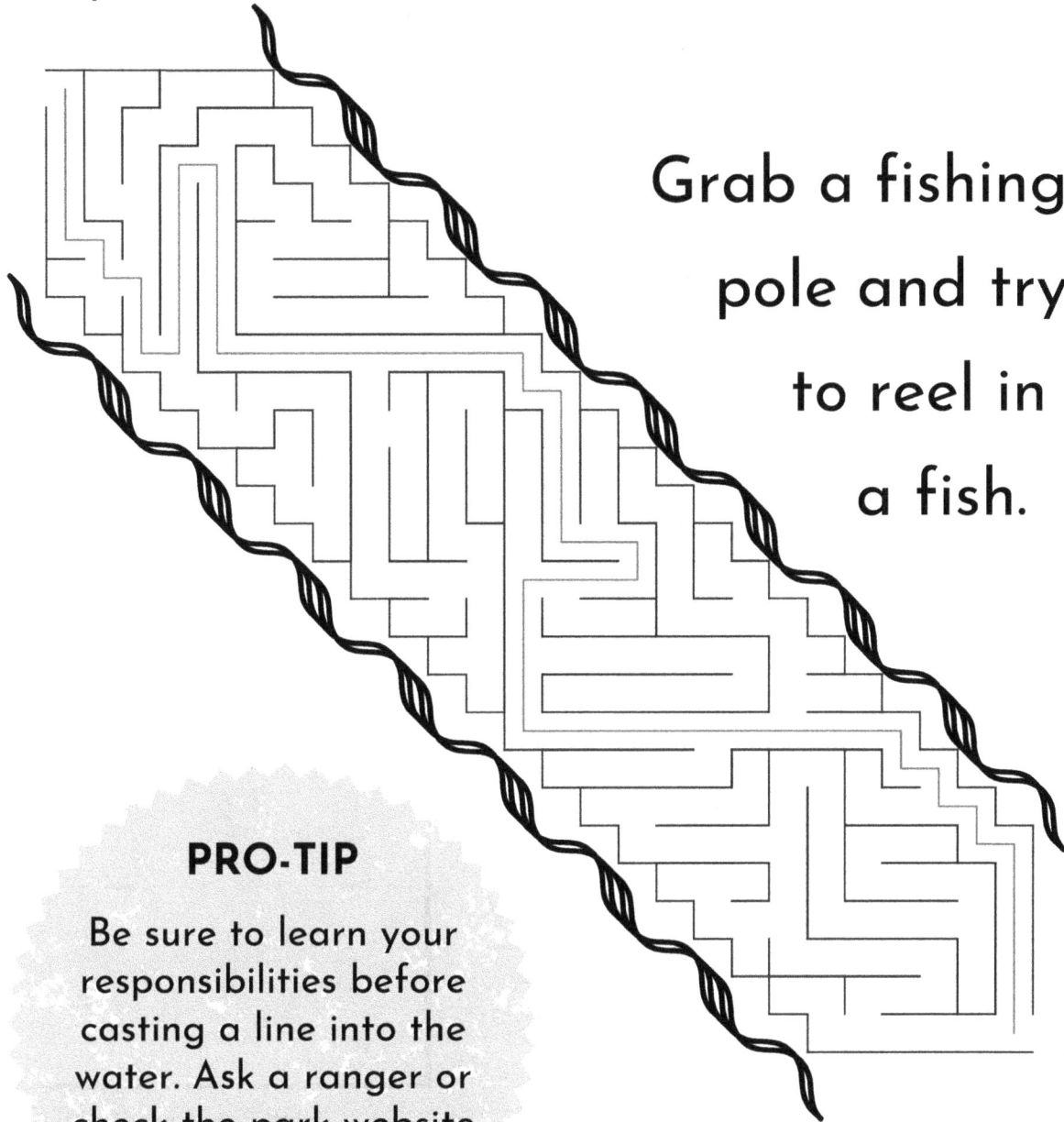

Grab a fishing pole and try to reel in a fish.

PRO-TIP

Be sure to learn your responsibilities before casting a line into the water. Ask a ranger or check the park website before you go.

Decoding Using American Sign Language

American Sign Language, also called ASL for short, is a language that many Deaf people or people who are hard of hearing use to communicate. People use ASL to communicate with their hands. Did you know people from all over the country and world travel to national parks? You may hear people speaking other languages. You might also see people using ASL. Use the American Manual Alphabet chart to decode some national parks facts.

This was the first national park to be established:

Y E L L O W S T O N E

This is the biggest national park in the US:

W R A N G E L L -

S T .   E L I A S

This is the most visited national park:

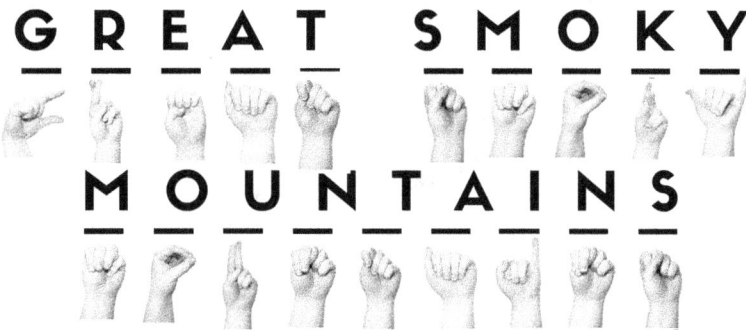

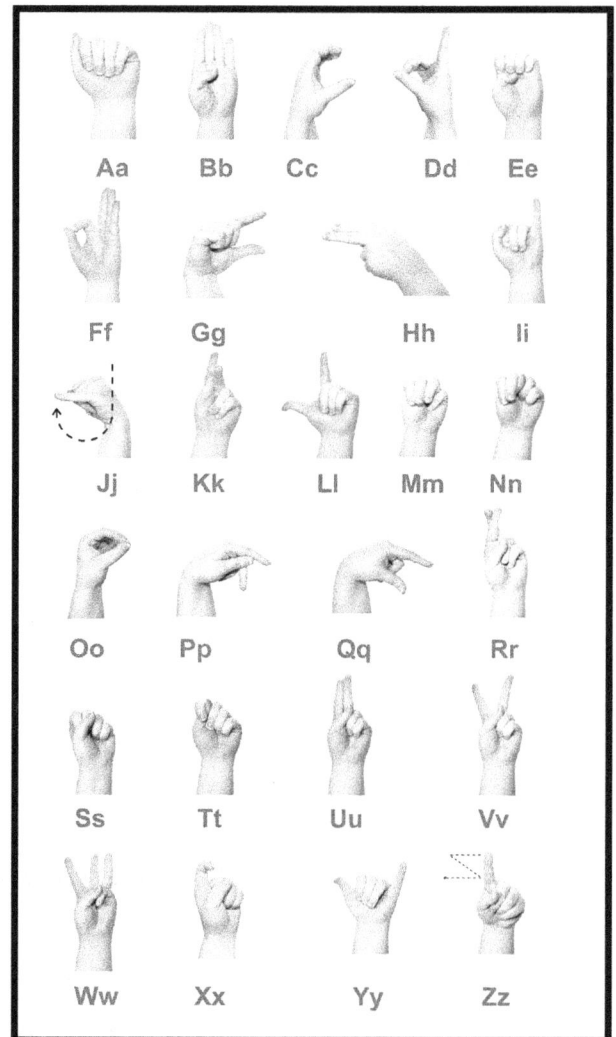

G R E A T   S M O K Y

M O U N T A I N S

Aa	Bb	Cc	Dd	Ee
Ff	Gg		Hh	Ii
Jj	Kk	Ll	Mm	Nn
Oo	Pp		Qq	Rr
Ss	Tt	Uu		Vv
Ww	Xx	Yy	Zz	

Hint: Pay close attention to the position of the thumb!

Try it! Using the chart, try to make the letters of the alphabet with your hand. What is the hardest letter to make? Can you spell out your name? Show a friend or family member and have them watch you spell out the name of the national park you are in.

Go Birdwatching at Wheeler Peak Campground

start
here

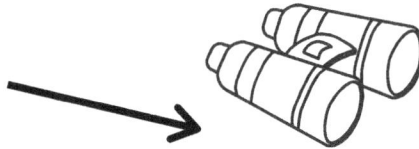

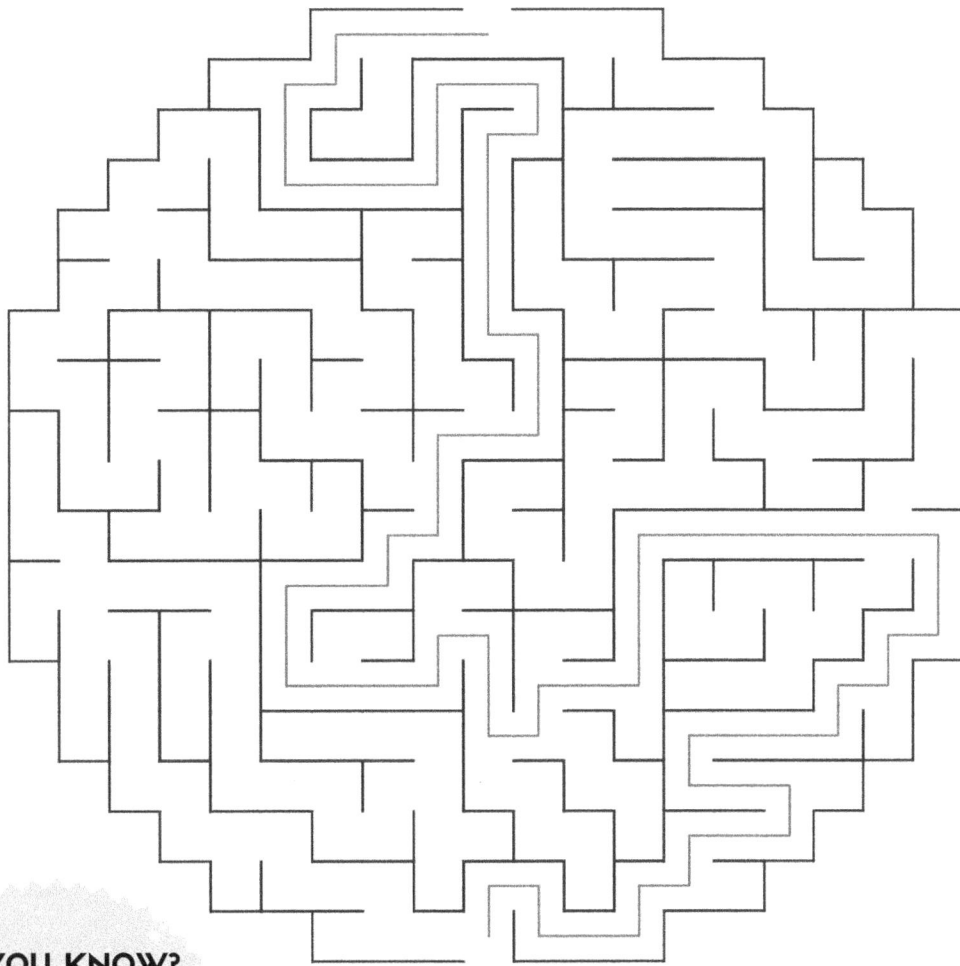

DID YOU KNOW?
Great Basin NP is home to several birds of prey, including eagles, hawks, and owls. Birds of prey are birds that hunt other animals for food.

Let's Go Camping at Baker Creek

1. tent
2. camp stove
3. sleeping bag
4. bug spray
5. sunscreen
6. map
7. flashlight
8. pillow
9. lantern
10. ice
11. snacks
12. smores
13. water
14. first aid kit
15. chair
16. cards
17. books
18. games
19. trail
20. hat

```
D P P I L L O W D B T E A C I
E O A D P R E A A M B R C A N
P W C A M P S T O V E I H X G
R A H S G E L E B E E D A P S
E L B U G S P R A Y N G I E A
S I A H G C I C N N M E R C N
C W N L A F I R S K O O B F K
M T A E M I L E L H M R W L J
T A P R E A O R E S L B A A B
S M P A S R R T E N T L U S C
C E A I I R C G P E I U J H A
S S N A C K S S I M O K I L R
I J R S F O I S N J R A Q I D
C Y E T L E V E G U O R V G S
E W T A K C A B B S S O H H M
X J N F I R S T A I D K I T T
U A A E S S E N G E T P V A B
C J L I A R T D N A M A H A S
```

68

All in the Day of a Park Ranger

There are many right answers for this activity, but not all of the provided examples are good activities for a park ranger. In fact, a park ranger's job may include stopping visitors from doing some of these things.

The list below are activities that rangers do not do:

feed the migratory birds

throw rocks off the side of the mountain

pick wildflowers

share marshmallows with squirrels

catch frogs or toads and make them race

What are Reptiles?

1.   Lizard

2.   Snake

3.   Skink

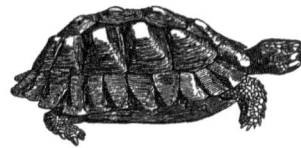

4.   Tortoise

Answers: Other National Parks Crossword

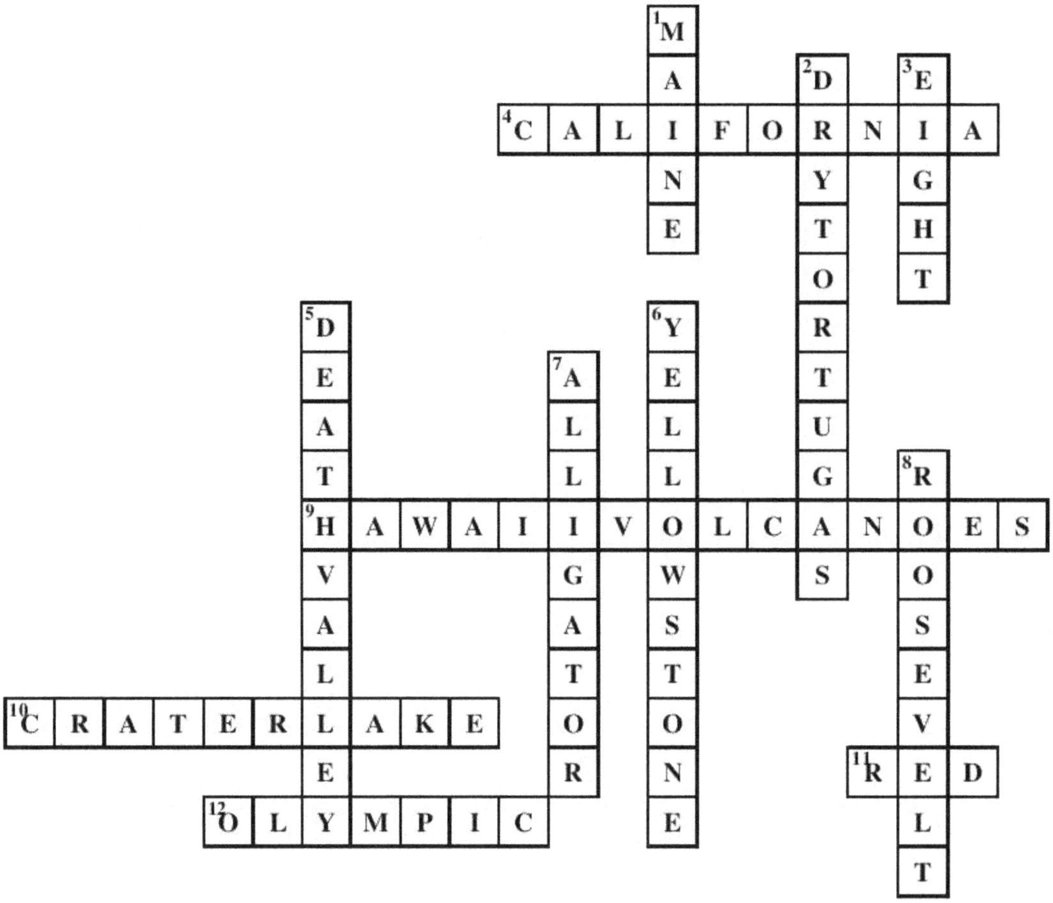

1 MAINE
2 DRYTORTUGAS
3 EIGHT
4 CALIFORNIA
5 DEATHVALLEY
6 YELLOWSTONE
7 ALLIGATOR
8 ROOSEVELT
9 HAWAIIVOLCANOES
10 CRATERLAKE
11 RED
12 OLYMPIC

Down

1. State where Acadia National Park is located
2. This National Park has the Spanish word for turtle in it
3. Number of National Parks in Alaska
5. This National Park has some of the hottest temperatures in the world
6. This National Park is the only one in Idaho
7. This toothsome creature can famously be found in Everglades National Park
8. Only president with a national park named for them

Across

4.This state has the most National Parks
9.This park has some of the newest land in the US, caused by a volcanic eruption
10. This park has the deepest lake in the United States
11. This color shows up in the name of a National Park in California
12.This National Park deserves a gold medal

Answers: Which National Park Will You Go To Next?

1. Zion
2. Big Bend
3. Glacier
4. Olympic
5. Sequoia
6. Bryce
7. Mesa Verde
8. Biscayne
9. Wind Cave
10. Great Basin
11. Katmai
12. Yellowstone
13. Voyageurs
14. Arches
15. Badlands
16. Denali
17. Glacier Bay
18. Hot Springs

```
F  M  M  E  S  A  V  E  R  D  E  B  N  E  Y
E  A  B  I  G  B  E  N  D  E  S  A  S  E  M
Y  L  I  C  A  L  O  Y  N  E  E  D  L  T  G
D  M  G  A  S  S  A  U  C  N  R  L  U  E  R
C  E  L  I  I  T  S  C  R  E  O  A  A  K  E
S  N  A  W  Y  E  E  O  I  W  T  N  A  C  A
G  I  C  H  A  A  Q  C  S  E  M  D  N  S  T
N  O  I  Z  P  R  U  T  I  M  R  S  N  E  B
I  W  E  L  M  P  O  N  B  W  E  B  K  H  A
R  J  R  F  D  N  I  F  L  I  H  B  U  C  S
P  A  B  E  E  S  A  N  E  S  O  P  W  R  I
S  J  A  E  N  Y  A  C  S  I  B  A  U  A  N
T  C  Y  I  A  D  O  H  H  Y  M  E  A  L  R
O  T  A  T  L  M  L  E  S  E  G  R  W  R  J
H  S  T  O  I  K  A  T  M  A  I  R  O  P  B
I  C  H  U  R  C  O  L  Y  M  P  I  C  O  U
O  Y  G  T  S  D  E  O  S  B  R  Y  C  E  T
W  I  N  D  C  A  V  E  I  N  R  O  H  E  M
```

LITTLE BISON
Press

Little Bison Press is an independent children's book publisher based in the Pacific Northwest. We promote exploration, conservation, and adventure through our books. Established in 2021, our passion for outside spaces and travel inspired the creation of Little Bison Press.

We seek to publish books that support children in learning about and caring for the natural places in our world.

To learn more, visit:
www.littlebisonpress.com

Want more free games and activities? Visit our website!

www.ingramcontent.com/pod-product-compliance
Lightning Source LLC
Chambersburg PA
CBHW080426030426
42335CB00020B/2609